THE JONAS BROTHERS

Mitchell Lane
PUBLISHERS

P.O. Box 196
Hockessin, Delaware 19707
Visit us on the web: www.mitchelllane.com
Comments? email us: mitchelllane@mitchelllane.com

Mitchell Lane PUBLISHERS

Printing   6   7   8   9

A Robbie Reader
Contemporary Biography

Abigail Breslin	Albert Pujols	Alex Rodriguez
Aly and AJ	Amanda Bynes	Ashley Tisdale
Brenda Song	Brittany Murphy	Charles Schulz
Dakota Fanning	Dale Earnhardt Jr.	David Archuleta
Demi Lovato	Donovan McNabb	Drake Bell & Josh Peck
Dr. Seuss	Dwayne "The Rock" Johnson	Dylan & Cole Sprouse
Eli Manning	Emily Osment	Hilary Duff
Jaden Smith	Jamie Lynn Spears	Jesse McCartney
Jimmie Johnson	Johnny Gruelle	Jonas Brothers
Jordin Sparks	LeBron James	Mia Hamm
Miley Cyrus	Miranda Cosgrove	Raven-Symone
Selena Gomez	Shaquille O'Neal	Story of Harley-Davidson
Syd Hoff	Tiki Barber	Tom Brady
Tony Hawk		

Library of Congress Cataloging-in-Publication Data
Mattern, Joanne, 1963–
Jonas Brothers / by Joanne Mattern.
    p. cm. — (A Robbie reader)
Includes bibliographical references, discography and index.
ISBN 978-1-58415-721-2 (library bound)
1. Jonas Brothers (Musical group) — Juvenile literature. 2. Rock musicians — United States — Biography — Juvenile literature. I. Title.
ML3930.J62M38 2009
782.42164092'2 — dc22
[B]
                                                         2008008076

ABOUT THE AUTHOR: Joanne Mattern is the author of more than 250 books for children. She has written biographies about many famous people for Mitchell Lane Publishers, including *Peyton Manning, Ashley Tisdale, LeBron James,* and *Drake Bell and Josh Peck.* Joanne also enjoys writing about animals, reading, and being outdoors. She lives in New York State with her husband, four children, and several pets.

PUBLISHER'S NOTE: The following story has been thoroughly researched and to the best of our knowledge represents a true story. While every possible effort has been made to ensure accuracy, the publisher will not assume liability for damages caused by inaccuracies in the data, and makes no warranty on the accuracy of the information contained herein. This story is not authorized or endorsed by the Jonas Brothers.

PLB / PLB2 / PLB2,10 / PLB2 / PLB2,28,29 / PLB2,28,29

TABLE OF CONTENTS

Words in **bold** type can be found in the glossary.

Kevin, Nick, and Joe Jonas started singing and playing music together when they were kids. By 2007, they were one of the most popular bands among children and teens.

A Scary Discovery

In March 2007, about 1,000 people gathered in New York City to raise money for the **Diabetes** Research Institute's Carnival for a Cure. Diabetes is a serious disease. If a person has diabetes, his or her body cannot make a chemical called **insulin**. Insulin helps the body change the sugar in food into energy.

The people at the carnival were thrilled when the Jonas Brothers got up to perform. The three brothers in the band sang their hit songs, including "Mandy" and "Time for Me to Fly." The crowd went wild. Nicholas Jonas, the youngest member of the band, stepped up to the microphone. "How many people here have diabetes?" he asked. A lot of hands went

When Nick was thirteen, he began to feel tired all the time. Doctors discovered he had diabetes. Nick refuses to let diabetes stop him from performing. He has worked to help others with this disease.

up. Many of the people who raised their hands were children.

Then, Nick surprised everyone: He put up his hand too. For the first time, Nick told the world that he had diabetes. He learned he had the disease in 2005.

When he found out he had diabetes, Nick was very scared. "I wondered, 'Why me?' Then I asked myself, 'Why not me?' and realized that I might be able to help other kids with diabetes," he said.

6

The Jonas Brothers became famous in 2006, when they released their first CD. Young fans love their energetic music, good looks, and fun personalities.

Nick will not let diabetes stop him from enjoying his life. "I want to let kids know that it doesn't have to be so hard," he said. "The most important thing is to never ever let yourself get down about having diabetes, because you can live a really great life."

Nick and his brothers are certainly having a really great life. They are one of the most popular bands in America.

The Jonas Brothers know that being brothers makes them closer than members of other bands. "We love what we're doing and we want to do it for a long while," says Nick.

From New Jersey to Broadway

On November 5, 1987, Kevin and Denise Jonas welcomed their first child, Paul Kevin Jonas Jr. Their second child, Joseph Adam, was born on August 15, 1989. A few years later, on September 16, 1992, Nicholas Jerry joined them. Kevin, Joe, and Nick also have a younger brother, Frankie. The boys grew up in the quiet town of Wyckoff (WY-kof), New Jersey.

Kevin and Denise Jonas are both musicians, and music was always a big part of the family's life. The family often performed in church.

Joe, Nick, and Kevin hang out with their younger brother, Frankie. They call Frankie "the Bonus Jonas" and expect he will join their band when he is older. He will also appear with them in *J.O.N.A.S.!*

Nick started singing almost as soon as he learned how to talk. "From the time I was two years old, I would wake up in the morning and start singing all the time, every second of the day," he said.

One day, Nick climbed on top of a coffee table and started singing. When his grandmother told him to get down, Nick told her, "No, Grandma, I need to practice. I'm going to be on **Broadway**."

When Nick was about five years old, he started watching **musicals**. "I watched *Peter Pan* five times a day," he said. "I would watch every single movement—the dancing, how they acted, how their mouths moved when they sang."

All that practice paid off. One day, six-year-old Nick and his mother were at the barber shop. As Nick got his hair cut, he started to sing. A woman in the shop told Denise that Nick should be on Broadway. She gave Denise the name of a person who **managed** Broadway performers.

Denise brought Nick and Joe to **audition** for the manager. He liked them and agreed to find work for them. Soon the boys appeared in Broadway shows, including *A Christmas Carol* and *Annie Get Your Gun*. The brothers' rise to fame was just beginning.

The brothers enjoy performing for their fans. "It's awesome. It never gets old," says Joe.

Disney Comes Calling

Nick appeared in several Broadway shows. One of his favorite roles was Chip in *Beauty and the Beast*. Nick loved being on Broadway. "It's awesome. I love everything about it," he said. "It's so exciting to go on stage every day—to sing a song and know 1,500 people are watching!"

However, being on Broadway was also a lot of hard work. Nick spent forty hours a week **rehearsing**, performing, and traveling back and forth to New York City. It was impossible to stay in school. His mother decided to homeschool all her children. This way, the boys could learn *and* perform.

13

The brothers are close to their mom, Denise. Mom and Dad always travel with the band and stay near their sons.

When Nick was in *Beauty and the Beast,* the **cast** of the show was asked to sing a Christmas song. The song would be on a CD that would raise money for **charity**. Nick and his father wrote a song called "Joy to the World (A Christmas Prayer)." The song became a big hit on radio stations that played Christian music.

The record company, Columbia, wanted Nick to record more songs. Nick, Joe, and Kevin wrote a song together called "Please Be Mine." When the people at Columbia heard the song, they knew Nick was not the only star in the family. They asked Joe and Kevin to come for an audition. "All three of us were signed pretty much on the spot as the Jonas Brothers," Kevin explained. Nick and Joe both sang and played guitar, keyboards, and drums. Kevin played lead guitar and also sang.

The Jonas Brothers went on **tour**. They played all over the United States. The band opened for such stars as Jesse McCartney, Kelly Clarkson, the Click Five, and the Backstreet Boys. Fans loved them!

When Radio Disney began playing the Jonas Brothers' songs, even more young people heard them perform. They liked what they heard!

In August 2006, the Jonas Brothers released their first CD, called *It's About Time*. A favorite song on the album, "Mandy," is about a girl who was taught sign language by Denise

In 2006, Radio Disney began playing more songs by the Jonas Brothers. The JoBros want their music to appeal to all ages, from young to old.

Jonas. "We were writing songs one day and decided we wanted to write about something really nice, so we wrote a song about Mandy," Nick said. "She's the nicest girl you'll ever meet." In fact, many of the songs are about things that have happened to the brothers. "It's not stuff that we don't know about," Nick said.

It's About Time was very successful. The songs on the CD were played on MTV and Radio Disney, and the song "Year 3000" reached the Top 40 radio charts.

However, things were changing at the band's record company. The people who had signed the boys did not work there anymore. The boys left Columbia in December 2006. They quickly signed up with Hollywood Records, which is owned by Disney.

"Disney has found a way to unlock the door," said the boys' father. Indeed, the band was about to become very famous—Disney-style!

Kevin, Nick, and Joe wave to fans in Mexico City in April 2008. The brothers have appeared all over the world.

Superstars!

The year 2007 was big for the Jonas Brothers. In August, the group's second CD, called *Jonas Brothers,* was released. The CD was a huge hit. It entered the Billboard Top 200 chart at number five. The Billboard charts track sales and radio airplay for songs and CDs.

Later that year, the Jonas Brothers went on tour all over the United States. They were thrilled to be the opening act for Miley Cyrus, another hot young Disney star. She has her own TV show, *Hannah Montana.* Miley and the Jonas Brothers became good friends. They spent a lot of time listening to music and playing video games together. The brothers even appeared on her show.

The Jonas Brothers were thrilled to tour with Miley Cyrus. They had a lot of fun during that time. "We're good friends," Nick says.

The brothers made several other television appearances during 2007. They performed at the Miss Teen USA contest and the Disney Channel Games. In November, they played their single "S.O.S." at the American Music Awards. Nick, Joe, and Kevin also appeared in the Macy's Thanksgiving Day Parade. On New Year's Eve, they performed several songs in New York's Times Square.

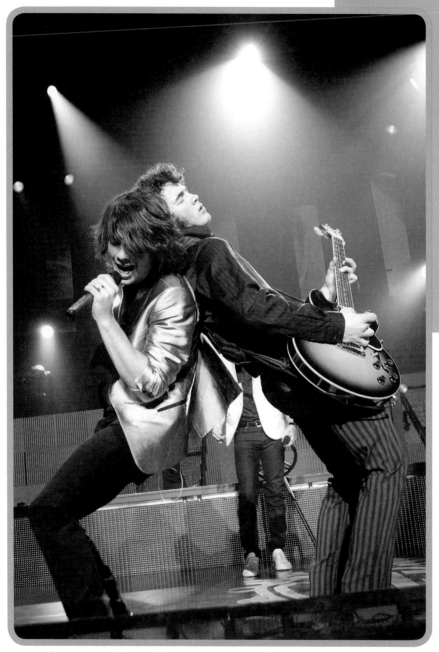

Joe and Kevin rock out during a concert. The brothers grew up in a musical family and enjoy many different kinds of music.

The Jonas Brothers also found fame on the Internet site YouTube. The band makes many videos and puts them on YouTube for everyone to see. It is a great way for their fans to see them even when they are not on tour.

Nick, Joe, and Kevin are busy performing and recording music, but they have not forgotten to help others. The brothers give 10 percent of their **income** to churches and charities.

Nick continues to help children who have diabetes. He and his brothers also raise money for Nick's **foundation**, Nicholas Jonas Change for the Children. Its goal is to help poor, homeless, and seriously ill children. Nick decided to start the foundation in 2002, when he saw a homeless family on a New York City street.

The brothers and their family are also very active in church activities. They are all Christians and work hard to keep their faith strong. They also try to set a good example for others. Nick feels that he and his brothers try to live as God wants them to. "I just want to do

The Jonas Brothers pose with young fans at an event to encourage young people to think about the environment. The JoBros love meeting fans and know they are lucky to be so popular.

whatever the Lord has planned for me to do," he told *Clubhouse* magazine.

The brothers found many new fans when their song "Kids of the Future"
was featured in the 2007 Disney movie *Meet the Robinsons*.

A Bright Future

In 2007, the Jonas Brothers' song "Kids of the Future" was featured in the movie *Meet the Robinsons.* The brothers are kids of the future themselves. The band has big plans.

Disney would continue to bring the Jonas Brothers to television, and asked them to make a 2008 concert special. They appeared in *Hannah Montana/Miley Cyrus: Best of Both Worlds Concert Tour.* Disney would also make a reality series about their lives. That series, called *Jonas Brothers: Living the Dream,* follows the brothers both on and off the stage. The brothers also starred in a 2008 Disney Channel movie, *Camp Rock,* and would play a group of spies in a Disney Channel series called *J.O.N.A.S.!* Meanwhile, as the brothers were working on their third album, they continued their music tour.

Denise and Kevin Jonas want their sons to be normal kids, so they travel with them on tour, along with younger brother Frankie. A teacher also travels with the band so that Nick can keep up with his schoolwork. Kevin and Joe have already finished high school.

The brothers know that being a family is an important part of their success. "As brothers, we just know how to work together," Nick says. "It's awesome to have my brothers on stage and in the **studio** with me. You have a security that everything is going to be okay, even when you mess up."

Joe agrees that the brothers will work together for a long time. "We're brothers, so it's not like, if we got upset at each other that we can be like, 'Well, I quit.' They're still my brothers. We love to do this and we know we're going to keep doing it for a very long time."

In April 2008, Kevin, Joe, and Nick were invited to the annual White House Correspondents' Association Dinner as guests of President George W. Bush. When the JoBros arrived, the crowd outside the White House went wild. "It's crazy, Nick said. "We never expected this."

Nick, Joe, and Kevin know that they are living a great life. "We wake up every morning excited because we get to do what we love," Kevin says. "Our dreams have really come true and we're just so lucky."

CHRONOLOGY

1987   Paul Kevin Jonas Jr. is born on November 5.

1989   Joseph Adam Jonas is born on August 15.

1992   Nicholas Jerry Jonas is born on September 16.

1999   Nick begins appearing in Broadway shows.

2002   Nick and his father write and record a song called "Joy to the World (A Christmas Prayer)." Nick starts his foundation, Nicholas Jonas Change for the Children.

2004   Nick is signed to Columbia Records.

2005   Columbia signs Nick, Joe, and Kevin as a band; the group decides to call itself the Jonas Brothers. They go on several tours; their first single, "Mandy," is released. Nick is diagnosed with diabetes.

2006   The Jonas Brothers' first CD, *It's About Time,* is released. Columbia drops the band; they sign with Hollywood Records.

2007   The band's second CD, *Jonas Brothers,* is released; they make many TV appearances and tour with Miley Cyrus.

2008   The Jonas Brothers appear in the Disney concert special *Hannah Montana/Miley Cyrus: Best of Both Worlds Concert Tour* with Miley Cyrus, and in the Disney movie *Camp Rock.* Their third CD, *A Little Bit Longer,* debuts at #1 on the Billboard chart. The brothers also star in their own Disney series, *J.O.N.A.S.!* They work on their reality series, *Jonas Brothers: Living the Dream.*

2009   A movie of their Burning Up tour, *Jonas Brothers: The 3D Concert Experience,* is released in February, along with the movie's sound track. The brothers begin World Tour 2009, which sells more than one million tickets in the first week. *Lines, Vines and Trying Times* debuts at #1 on the Billboard chart.

DISCOGRAPHY

Albums

2009   *Lines, Vines and Trying Times*
           Music From the 3D Concert Experience

2008   *A Little Bit Longer*

2007   *Jonas Brothers*
           Jonas Brothers: Bonus Jonas Edition

2006   *It's About Time*

Hit Singles

"Paranoid"

"Burning Up"

"Mandy"

"S.O.S."

"Year 3000"

FILMOGRAPHY

2009   *Jonas Brothers: The 3D Concert Experience*

2008   *J.O.N.A.S.!*
           Camp Rock
           Hannah Montana/Miley Cyrus: Best of Both Worlds Concert Tour

FIND OUT MORE

Books

Johns, Michael-Anne. *Jonas Brothers Unauthorized* (Star Scene). New York: Scholastic, 2008.

Leavitt, Amie Jane. *Miley Cyrus.* Hockessin, Delaware: Mitchell Lane Publishers, 2008.

Ryals, Lexi. *Jammin' with the Jonas Brothers: An Unauthorized Biography.* New York: Price Stern Sloan, 2008.

FIND OUT MORE

Works Consulted

Children with Diabetes: "Nick Jonas Reveals He Has Diabetes." http://www.childrenwithdiabetes.com/pressreleases/dri20070311.htm

Cotliar, Sharon. "The Jumping Jonas Brothers." *People Weekly,* January 21, 2008, p. 79.

Hadley, Suzanne. "Star Bright." http://www.clubhousemagazine.com/truelife/interviews/a0001236.cfm

Jackson, Vincent. "Three New Jersey Guys Upstage a Disney Queen." http://www.pressofatlanticcity.com/top_three/story/7525709p-7426898c.html

Orr, Amanda. "Jonas Bros. 'Didn't Expect' White House Dinner Reaction." *People,* April 27, 2008. http://www.people.com/people/article/0,,20195769,00.html

Starpulse.com: "Jonas Brothers Biography." http://www.starpulse.com/Music/Jonas_Brothers/Biography/

Tiger Beat. June 2008.

On the Internet

Disney
  http://www.disney.com

The Jonas Brothers
  http://www.jonasbrothers.com

GLOSSARY

audition (aw-DIH-shun)—To try out for a part in a play, concert, or movie.

Broadway (BRAWD-way)—Theaters in New York City.

cast (KAST)—The group of people who perform in a play or movie.

charity (CHAIR-uh-tee)—An organization that helps people in need.

diabetes (dy-uh-BEE-teez)—A disease that prevents the body from processing sugar properly.

foundation (fown-DAY-shun)—An organization that raises money for charities.

income (IN-kum)—The amount of money a person makes.

insulin (IN-suh-lin)—A chemical that helps the body process sugar.

managed (MAN-ehjd)—Took charge of someone's work or career.

musicals (MYOO-zih-kulz)—Plays or movies that include singing and dancing.

rehearsing (ruh-HER-sing)—Practicing for a performance.

studio (STOO-dee-oh)—A place to record music.

tour (TOOR)—A trip to different places to perform.

INDEX